Tor

THE V… S

EAST SIDE

published 30 years ago
gives a 'look-in'
"Before Modern Era"

Many areas now "out
of bounds"/off-limits

Rosemary Neering

WHITECAP BOOKS
Vancouver/Toronto

The information in this book is true and complete to the best of our
knowledge. All recommendations are made without guarantee on the
part of the author or Whitecap Books Ltd. The author and publisher
disclaim any liability in connection with the use of this information.
For additional information please contact Whitecap Books Ltd.,
1086 West Third Street, North Vancouver, B.C., V7P 3J6.

Edited by Elizabeth McLean
Cover design by Warren Clark
Interior design by Susan Doering
Map by Stuart Daniel, Starshell Maps
Cover photograph by Ryan McNair
Interior photographs are by the author, except where otherwise indicated.
Archival photographs courtesy of BCARS (British Columbia Archives and
Records Services); CVA (City of Vancouver Archives).
Typeset by CryptoGraphics

Printed and bound in Canada.

Canadian Cataloguing in Publication Data

Neering, Rosemary, 1945–
   The Vancouver walking guides: East side

   ISBN 1-55110-143-2
   1. Vancouver (B.C.)—Guidebooks. 2. Walking—British Columbia—
Vancouver—Guidebooks. I. Title.
FC3847.18.N442 1994   917.11'33   C94-910013-7
F1089.5.V22N442 1994

CONTENTS

INTRODUCTION

THE SUN SHINES brightly this summer morning on a dozen elderly Japanese Canadians, garbed in sporting white, who whack balls through hoops set up on the grass of Oppenheimer Park. On two benches nearby, a clutch of east-siders, chins stubbly, clothes wrinkled and worn, tilt bottles of cheap wine in brown paper bags and watch gate ball, the Far Eastern version of croquet.

Elsewhere in Vancouver, the scene might raise eyebrows. But not here: this park has seen turn-of-the-century baseball games, open-air fish markets, bitter Depression-era rallies of the unemployed, pensioners escaping from their tiny rooms to talk with friends, late-night drug deals. That the same city block has room in the 1990s for both a celebration of Japanese culture and the poorest Vancouverites is here no contradiction.

The unemployed and their supporters crowd Oppenheimer Park to protest police brutality after men were evicted from the Vancouver Post Office in 1938. (BCARS 55527)

For Oppenheimer Park is a microcosm of Vancouver's East Side, a district that has long been home to generations of new immigrants, blue-collar workers, and people down on their luck. From Chinatown to Strathcona to the docks, this district wears no cosmetics, puts on no airs. Lively, colourful, sometimes seamy, it provides one of Vancouver's most interesting walking tours.

The City of Vancouver began on the East Side. In 1865, Edward Stamp established Hastings Mill at the present foot of Dunlevy Street, the first non-native settlement on the south shore of Burrard Inlet. After the Canadian Pacific Railway reached down the inlet in 1887 to the neighbouring settlement of Gastown, renamed Vancouver, land south of the mill was surveyed and cleared, streets were laid out, and houses were built. This area, between Main Street and present-day Clark Drive, from the waterfront to False Creek, became known as Strathcona.

At first, this district housed Vancouver's well-off: the mayor, the mill manager, the best-known politicians and industrialists. But, by the turn of the century, they had moved west to newer, flashier neighbourhoods, and their homes had been converted to rooming houses. Near the docks, factories were established and warehouses built to serve the railway and the port. Between the docks and False Creek—then still a muddy tidal flat that reached the back door of Chinatown—small houses and large, stores and restaurants, rooming houses and hotels, churches and schools, bars and brothels, took shape in what had become the largely working-class neighbourhood of Strathcona.

Each succeeding working-class immigrant group that arrived in Vancouver—Chinese, Japanese, Ukrainians, Russians, Jews, Italians, Greeks—made their homes in Strathcona until each, in turn, moved on to other parts of the city.

In the 1880s, thousands of Chinese men were brought to British Columbia to work on the railroad. Once construction was complete they gravitated to Vancouver, living there part of the year and spending the rest working in logging camps, canneries, mills, and on farms and ranches. They congregated in Chinatown, along Pender Street on either side of Carrall, crowded there partly by the hostility of white Vancouver, partly because Chinatown contained the restaurants where they were allowed to eat, the rooming houses that would take them in, and the fraternal and benevolent societies that supported them. An anti-Asian riot in 1907 reinforced the separateness of Chinatown. Chinese immigration to Canada was virtually forbidden between 1923 and 1947; when it resumed, Chinatown expanded into the residential district to the east, and Strathcona became a largely Chinese neighbourhood.

By then, time and poverty had taken their toll in Strathcona, and it and the rest of the East Side had become increasingly run-down. In the 1950s, the answer to what was termed urban blight was urban renewal. City planners and city council proposed and began a massive scheme to demolish much of Strathcona and build block after block of identical apartment buildings and townhouses. They began the demolition—after all, said one planner, "Nobody cares about Strathcona but the people who live there"—but were halted by a vocal coalition of neighbourhood groups, heritage preservationists, and others who suggested that the existing eclectic mix of housing and people had far more value than the imposed and sterile environment of a rebuilt neighbourhood.

Chinatown was also threatened, by plans for freeways that would have destroyed much of the historic area. Those plans too were fought to a standstill and historic Chinatown was preserved. In the 1990s, the area faces a new challenge: its designation as historic has made it expensive and sometimes impossible for buildings to be renovated or the streetscape updated. Some Chinese Canadians now fear that Chinatown will be killed as anything other than a tourist attraction by the very designation meant to save it.

Through the centre of the East Side runs Hastings Street, some parts of it rightly dubbed skid road. Ever since logging camps existed upcoast, loggers on a city furlough have disembarked from ships at the nearby docks and made a beeline for the hotels, bars, and brothels of the area. Between Hastings and the waterfront, those hotels and bars still exist, along with missions, and what remains of the Japanese district of Vancouver along Powell Street. This district of Japanese-Canadian restaurants, stores, hotels, and bathhouses was almost destroyed when Japanese Canadians were exiled from the coast in 1942, but is now brought alive again each year by Japanese-Canadian festivals. In this area north of Hastings are also new blocks of subsidized housing, renovated and increasingly trendy warehouses, and the piers and wharves of Vancouver's port.

THE WALKING TOUR

THIS TOUR STARTS in the old blocks of Chinatown, moves through the newer blocks that have provided a commercial centre for Chinese Canadians since 1947, turns north to the old site of Hastings Mill, continues through what remains of the prewar Japanese enclave to Oppenheimer Park, then turns north again to travel through the warehouse and working port area. Walkers then go south into residential Strathcona, and return through Chinatown to the starting point. Six to seven kilometres long and relatively flat, it can be walked at a reasonable pace, without stops, in under two hours; with time for coffee, lunch, shopping, and relaxation, it can take half a day—or a full day.

To reach the starting point at the corner of West Pender and Carrall streets: The Stadium SkyTrain station is a long two and a half blocks away: from the station, walk north (toward the mountains) on Beatty Street, then turn right (east) on Pender. Or, take the #19 or #22 bus from downtown east along Pender Street to Carrall. There are a number of pay parking lots in and near Chinatown; the Downtown Parking Corporation (DPC) lot at Beatty and Pender is the most reasonably priced.

The tour begins with the busiest areas, then moves to quieter blocks, returns through Chinatown, and ends with a stop for rest and contemplation at the Dr. Sun Yat-Sen Garden. It can, of course, be followed in reverse.

Note: The tour does verge on downtown's skid road. Although I have walked it several times alone without feeling threatened, others may prefer to go with a companion or in a group. I would strongly recommend against walking the route—alone or otherwise—at night, though a stroll through Chinatown should present little problem.

Boldface numbers in the text refer to the map on pages 18–19.

Chinatown: Pender Street, Carrall to Gore

Begin at the southwest corner of West Pender and Carrall streets, outside 8 West Pender Street.

Vancouver's Chinatown dates from the 1880s, when some seventeen thousand Chinese came to British Columbia to work on the Canadian Pacific Railway line. Once the line—and the work—was finished, many came to Vancouver, living in the city when seasonal work up-coast and upcountry was finished or unavailable. Most lived, and most Chinese businesses were established, in the blocks along Pender from Carrall to Main streets. Like the rest of Vancouver, Chinatown was particularly busy in the decade after 1900; many of today's historic buildings date from those years.

Walk left (west) half a block along West Pender Street. The Shanghai Alley sign in front of you is all that remains of Shanghai and Canton alleys. Whites in Vancouver were hostile to Chinese from the beginning. In 1907, anti-Oriental feeling sent a white mob rampaging in Chinatown, smashing windows and threatening residents. After the riot, many Chinese retreated into the compounds that became known as Shanghai and Canton alleys. Many of the buildings along Shanghai Alley had two fronts: one that opened on the alley, a second (that could be quickly closed) on Carrall Street. Most of the buildings along the alleys were demolished in the 1940s; the two survivors, now almost derelict, face the massive new redevelopment scheme on the former Expo 86 lands.

Turn back and walk east on Pender. The long thin building at 8 West Pender **(1)** is well known as the narrowest commercial building in the world. Displayed in its windows are stories about its history. Chang Toy owned the Sam Kee Company, one of four commercial companies that dominated Chinese business life in Vancouver around the turn of the century. He erected the Sam Kee building after the city expropriated the front seven metres of this property, leaving him with a seemingly worthless sliver of land less than two metres deep. The ground floor is minuscule; the second storey, used as living quarters, was made larger by means of bay windows. The glass blocks in the sidewalk where you are standing allowed light into basement baths that extended almost to the street; the baths were used by Chinatown residents.

Across the street, on the northwest corner of West Pender and Carrall, the Chinese Freemasons Building (ca. 1901) is a combination of Chinese (Pender side) and western (Carrall side) architecture. Originally an anti-Manchu political party known as the Chee Kung Tong (CKT) of the Hongmen Society, the society established its first Canadian branch in Barkerville in 1863. Sun Yat-Sen, leading the fight to overthrow the Manchus, stayed in this building for several months in 1911, raising support and money for the battle overseas, and the CKT mortgaged the building to help support the fight. Sun Yat-Sen came to power in 1912 with the help of the National League Kuomintang (KMT). Their joint aim achieved, relations between the two groups turned sour, as the CKT resented the increasing influence wielded by the Kuomintang.

Interestingly, buildings erected by the two factions stand as bookends to Vancouver's Chinatown. The CKT, who changed their name to the Chinese Freemasons to encourage contact with whites, occupied this building at the western end, the Kuomintang one at the eastern end of the commercial district, at Pender and Gore.

The building on the northeast corner of East Pender (Pender splits into east and west sections at Carrall) and Carrall housed the *Chinese Times* from 1939 until 1993, when it closed shop, defeated by competing newspapers and increased integration of the Chinese community. Visible on both these buildings are cheater storeys: mezzanine floors between first and second floor, built because taxes were based on floor space and cheater storeys were not counted.

On the southeast corner of East Pender and Carrall are the gates and building of the Chinese Cultural Centre **(2)**. Planning for the centre at first united, then divided, then reunited often-warring factions in the Chinese-Canadian community. The architecture is said to have been inspired by Beijing's Imperial Palace; it includes recessed balconies and a second-floor walkway. The centre is built on a traditional north-south axis. Walk into the courtyard to enter the building, which houses a small bookstore devoted to books on Chinese and Chinese-Canadian culture and history. Guided walking tours of Chinatown are sometimes offered.

On facing walls at the entrance to the centre's courtyard are plaques commemorating Chinese railway workers and pioneers in Canada, and Chinese Canadians who died in the Canadian forces in World War II. Without evident irony, the war plaque suggests that their deaths helped all Chinese Canadians attain the citizens' rights finally given them in 1947.

The gate at the entrance to the courtyard was made in China, and moved here after Vancouver's Expo 86. Throughout Chinatown are colours and ornamentation that express Chinese heritage. This gate embodies many of these symbols: red for happiness, gold for wealth, and yellow to symbolize imperial power, are favourite colours, as is green, which can symbolize peace, growth, and harmony, or nature's bounty. Look on the gate for two of the great mythical animals of China: the dragon, which carries the spirit of China and symbolizes prosperity and supremacy; and the phoenix, which appears in time of peace. Other animals commonly represented are the unicorn, a good omen; and the lion, a symbol of valour. Look also for representations of pine, bamboo, and plum trees, for longevity; and of flowers that symbolize the four seasons—peony, lotus, chrysanthemum, and plum.

The Dr. Sun Yat-Sen Park and Garden is behind the Chinese Cultural Centre. For details, see page 43, at the end of this walking tour.

Pender Street from Carrall to Main **(3)** is lined with shops and restaurants. The buildings are both old and new, the oldest begun in 1889, the newest erected in the 1980s. The stores sell everything from cookware (Ming Wo's is a Vancouver tradition) to clothing to souvenirs. Check out the restaurants for dim sum, traditional Chinese brunch, usually served from 11 a.m. to 2 p.m. Servers wheel carts past your table; you point out what you want, and they add it to your bill. Specialties are steamed dumplings filled with shrimp or pork, fluffy barbecued

Buildings in the 100-block East Pender, with recessed balconies and cheater storeys.

pork buns, and more esoteric—to non-Chinese—offerings such as chicken feet and tripe. Look also for noodle/won ton houses, with pots of steaming noodles in the windows; these fast-food restaurants serve won ton, bowls of noodles with barbecued meats, and a variety of other quick, inexpensive dishes. If you are in Chinatown in the evening, look for restaurants serving Cantonese-style food (stir-fried, deep-fried, or steamed fish, vegetables, and meats), Mandarin/Peking-style (stronger flavours with dark soy), or Szechuan-style (hot and spicy).

Crowded sidewalks and trees make it difficult to see the features of buildings in these two blocks: it's probably better to get a general view from the opposite side of the street, then look close up for details outside and in. On the north side of the street (odd-numbered buildings), look for the Wing Sang building at 51–69 East Pender. Made up of a number of buildings, it contains the oldest (1889) remaining building in Chinatown; the date is inscribed above a cheater-storey door that opens into mid-air.

Turn left (north) at Columbia, then make an immediate right into the alleyway to see what remains of Market Alley, from 1900 on home to bakeries, laundries, and other Chinese businesses; in the 1940s Chinese ran cafés that catered to both Chinese and western appetites. Only the Green Door remains; the Orange and Red doors are long gone. Other cafés that front on the 100-block East Pender still serve this chow mein/lemon pie menu, now more typical of Chinese restaurants in small-town British Columbia.

Return to East Pender Street. Most Chinese immigrants came from a small area of southern China, bringing with them customs in architecture, food, and clothing. The recessed balconies evident on many buildings in these blocks are one such tradition. The balconies are cool in summer, warm in winter. They offer a vantage point over the street. Children play in them, clothes are hung to dry, and people gather to chat or view the passing parade.

Chinese who came to Canada continued the clan tradition: people with the same family name, or from the same area, or speaking the same dialect, joined together in mutual-help societies. The 1909 building at 108 East Pender was built by the Chinese Benevolent Association, formed by merchants in 1889, partly to support destitute railway workers. The association fought—rarely successfully until after World War II—anti-Chinese feelings in the city, provided help and support for Chinese Canadians, and tried to represent Chinese-Canadian views. The unusually tall Chin Wing Chun Society building at 160 East Pender and the Mon Keang School at 123 East Pender were built by societies or tongs. Chinese-language and culture studies began in the Mon Keang building in 1925. Look in this building for stained-glass windows inscribed with Chinese characters, and for a cheater storey.

This part of Chinatown, featuring mainly stores and restaurants, continues to Main Street, older and traditional buildings interspersed with newer ones. At Main Street, look left (north) to see, a block away, the domed Carnegie Library building, erected in 1902–3. Andrew Carnegie, an American industrialist who made his millions in steel, paid for libraries around the world, with the one proviso that they bear his name. The Vancouver library has long since decamped. The Carnegie building became the home of the Vancouver museum, then the Carnegie Centre, a community centre for the downtown East Side. It retains from library days the stained-glass portraits of Shakespeare, Robbie Burns, and Walter Scott.

Continue across Main on Pender. Visit this block **(4)** on a Sunday morning, and you'll be caught up in the closest that Vancouver comes to the crowded streets and markets of Hong Kong. Before 1947, Vancouver's Chinese community was largely male, workers brought here in the early years of the century, but unable to send for

Grocery shopping in Chinatown.

their wives and families. Once immigration curbs were lifted, women and children joined husbands and fathers, families immigrated together, and the Chinese community changed. A reflection of that change is visible in this block. On a busy day—and few days are quiet—elderly Chinese women and young Chinese-Canadian families share the crowded sidewalks with non-Chinese looking for the cheap, fresh, and different vegetables and fruits displayed on stalls that occupy half the sidewalk. Most produce is identified only by signs in Chinese, though some grocers provide translations. Inside the stores, preserved, canned, and dried foods share shelf space with cooking utensils. If you want to buy produce you're not familiar with, ask how to cook it: although service may be brusque on busy days, store staff can be helpful.

Shops in this block display barbecued pork, duck, and chicken, with Chinese sausage hanging in long strips alongside. In the 1970s, Vancouver's health officer demanded that these cooked meats be stored in special ovens or refrigerated. But the Committee to Save Chinese Barbecued Products finally won a protracted battle, through public relations and scientific evidence, to demonstrate that the products were safe. You can still buy duck and chicken by the half or whole, and barbecued pork by the piece: you can ask for them to be chopped into bite-sized pieces.

Also in this block and along Gore Street are fish markets, where fish and crustaceans are kept live in tanks until they are sold. Fresh and frozen fish and other delicacies such as squid and sea cucumber are available in season.

Stores and restaurants in this area show the changing nature of the Asian community in Vancouver: Vietnamese, many of them ethnic Chinese, many who arrived in Canada as refugees, run Vietnamese restaurants and staff a drop-in centre in this area.

At the corner of Gore Avenue and East Pender (296 East Pender) stands the second bookend reminder of past Chinese politics, the Kuomintang western head-quarters built in 1920. Designed by a Scottish architect, the building shows no traditional Chinese features.

Gore Avenue, East Pender to Powell

Turn left (north) on Gore Avenue, and walk past yet more Chinese greengrocers, fish markets, and general stores. The Hotel East, at 445 Gore, built in 1912, was one of many used as lodging by Chinese immigrants. Gore, the original road used to skid logs on their way to Hastings Mill, was a street before the Canadian Pacific Railway (CPR) survey of 1885 established the street grid; it lies at a slight angle to that grid.

The building at the northeast corner of Gore and Hastings **(5)** has made an interesting transition: built in 1949 as a Salvation Army Temple, it now houses the Gold Buddha Monastery and the Dharma Realm Buddhist Association. The army opened this temple in 1950 on the site of headquarters built in 1906; they sold the building to the Buddhists in 1982, when they moved to new headquarters in Burnaby. But the army's days in Vancouver go back to 1887, just after the city's birth, when four "hallelujah lassies" arrived in Vancouver, held open-air meetings and parades on Carrall Street near Cordova, and used Hart's Opera House as a meeting hall. Hallelujah Point, in Stanley Park, is so named because the women picnicked there, taking along flag, drum, and tambourine. The Buddhist centre and monastery is one of a number of Buddhist centres on the East Side.

Hastings Street has long been a major thoroughfare, the main west-east route between downtown Vancouver, Burnaby, and beyond. Some blocks and buildings between Gore and Granville attract the worst-off of East Side residents, giving merit to its skid-road designation. But the street retains some of the life it once had when it was at the commercial centre of the city.

Look left from Gore on Hastings (or walk half a block west on the north side of Hastings) to see some of old Hastings Street, the mecca for loggers taking a break from the woods. The Empress Hotel, 235 East Hastings, built in 1912 as a travellers' hotel, demonstrates what

Narrow hotels on Hastings Street, west of Gore.

can be done on a lot 7.6 metres wide. The Afton Hotel was also built in 1912. The Ovaltine Cafe **(6)** sports a fancy neon sign, a throwback to the 1940s; you can linger at the long counter over a cup of coffee and basic coffee-shop fare—or, surprisingly, eggs Benedict.

Continue north on Gore. 341 Gore began as the fraternal hall of the Grand Orange Lodge, became a wrestling arena, then was converted to emergency housing during the housing shortage of World War II. The Firehall Arts Centre on the left occupies the former headquarters of the Vancouver Fire Department, the last firehall built in Vancouver to house horse-drawn boiler wagons. Accessible from Gore, but fronting on Cordova Street, the Vancouver Police Museum is housed in the old Coroner's Court building. St. James Anglican Church **(7)** on the northeast corner of Gore and Cordova is unusual, with a massive, somewhat Gothic basilica and thick concrete walls. Note that the English architect who designed St. James had just designed a Cairo cathedral.

Powell Street to Oppenheimer Park

Continue north on Gore, then turn right (east) on Powell Street. Before World War II, this area **(8)** was a thriving Japanese-Canadian community, known to outsiders as Japantown or Little Tokyo, to Japanese Canadians simply as Powell Street. In 1907, anti-Orientalists rioted and destroyed property in Chinatown. When they

A photo opportunity at St. James Anglican Church.

reached Powell Street, they were faced with Japanese ready to defend their property; the rioters promptly retreated.

In 1942, the Canadian government decided that people of Japanese heritage living on the Pacific coast posed a threat to national security. These Japanese and Japanese Canadians were rounded up and dispatched to internment camps in the British Columbia interior. Their possessions were confiscated and sold to non-Japanese, often at derisory prices. This forced relocation destroyed Powell Street's ethnic character. Since the war, it has slowly grown back, but the Japanese area is much smaller than it was when two dozen Japanese restaurants, bathhouses, and an open-air fish and vegetable market lined both sides of Powell Street for several blocks. Now, several stores featuring fresh produce and Japanese delicacies and products, plus a restaurant or two, are located on the south side of the 300-block Powell. Daikon, burdock, lotus root, and many other fruits and vegetables are displayed outside; look for rice crackers, noodles, pickled vegetables, and tofu inside. Other stores sell a variety of products, from hand-printed rice paper to books and kimonos.

At the southwest corner of Powell and Dunlevy is the New World Hotel, built by Japanese-Canadian businessman Shinkichi Tamura just before World War I. Across the street, on the north side, a mail station, a pawn shop, and a seaman's store serve transients and sailors from the nearby port.

Oppenheimer Park **(9)**, across Dunlevy Street between Powell and Cordova, was born as the Powell Street Grounds, the first official playing fields in Vancouver. It was later named for David Oppenheimer, a financial rival of the CPR who backed East Side development while the CPR was steadily pushing land development farther west. Oppenheimer and his brothers were pioneer merchants in Victoria, Barkerville, and Vancouver; mayor of Vancouver from 1888 to 1891, David Oppenheimer presided over expansionary and prosperous years in the city's history, contributing no little himself to that expansion and prosperity.

It requires an effort of will now to see this park as it was in the 1930s. In 1936, when the Vancouver Parks

Watching a baseball game at Oppenheimer Park.

Board declared that Oppenheimer was the only park where political, religious, or other views could be publicly voiced, it was only recognizing the obvious. Oppenheimer was the staging point for many a Depression-era rally. The unemployed crowded the square as socialists, labour leaders, and other spokesmen vented their anger and called for action. Along Powell Street beside the park, Japanese Canadians tarried with their shopping baskets, prodding fruits and vegetables and checking the freshness of fish laid out on open-air stalls. Longshoremen waiting for a call from one of the nearby hiring halls lounged on the benches, and Asahi League teams played on the baseball diamonds.

In more recent years, the park became a gathering

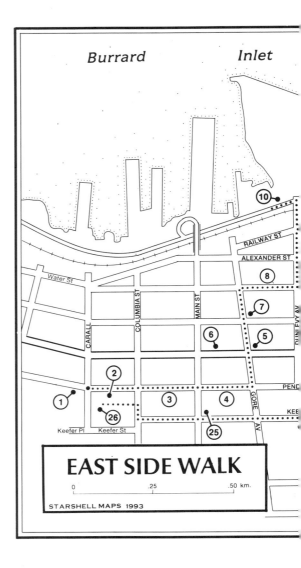

Burrard **Inlet**

RAILWAY ST

ALEXANDER ST

Water St

COLUMBIA ST

MAIN ST

CARRALL

DUNLEVY AV

⑩

⑧

⑦

⑥

⑤

① ② ③ ④

⑳

㉖

GORE AV

PEND

KEE

Keefer Pl   Keefer St

EAST SIDE WALK

0   .25   .50 km.

STARSHELL MAPS 1993

place for those on society's margins, and for the drug trade. Although neighbourhood residents and police are gradually succeeding in cleaning the area up, it's still not a good place to visit after dark. Panhandlers are rarely aggressive or difficult to deal with during daylight. A polite no (or some small change, if you are so inclined) and a smile will usually result in a friendly, "You have a nice day."

Oppenheimer Park used to be—and is becoming again—a focal point for the Japanese-Canadian community. The Powell Street Festival, held each August, shows the best of Japanese-Canadian culture as it exists today. Baseball teams and gate-ball enthusiasts often use the park for their sports. Where the footpaths cross in the middle of the park is a plaque set amid cherry trees; the words, translated as, "Looking back at home, I see smoke rising from kitchen fires," express the immigrant's nostalgia for Japan.

Opposite Oppenheimer Park on Powell Street is a row of false-fronted wooden buildings that date back to the 1890s.

Dunlevy Street and the Docks

At the corner of Powell and Dunlevy, turn north on Dunlevy Street, and walk toward the waterfront. Railway and Alexander streets, below Powell, are part of the warehouse district that grew up as wharves and piers were built along Vancouver's harbour. Empire Stevedoring, on the corner of Railway and Dunlevy, dates from 1941, but the tradition of stevedoring in Vancouver's port is much older. Although the distinction between stevedores and longshoremen is faint, in port parlance the stevedores were the employers of dock labour, the longshoremen. The first stevedores' union in Vancouver was formed in 1888; the longshoremen followed suit a few months later.

Look left (west) along Railway to see a line of warehouses used to receive and distribute goods arriving in or departing from Vancouver by sea. Several of these warehouses (329, 339, 343) date back to before World War I, while others were built in the 1940s. From the turn of the century to the 1950s, this was one of the busiest parts of town, as freight was warehoused for transfer between ship and train. But the trend to truck traffic created rapid change: warehouses were built on Vancouver's outskirts, and those near the rail lines and the port were used sparingly, allowed to fall derelict, or converted to other uses.

Cross the railway tracks on Dunlevy, and make an immediate left. This is an industrial area with no sidewalks, so watch for traffic, and be prepared to crowd in to the side of the road. On the right, beside the water, are the bright orange buildings of the Canadian Fishing Company (Canfisco) **(10)**, one of the few fish-packing and canning plants that remain of the dozens that once operated by the harbour and along the Fraser River. By 1949, Canfisco was the largest plant left on Vancouver's harbour. Women worked the canning lines in the 1940s

Fishing boats and the cannery at Canfisco.

for forty cents an hour, filleting and scaling; the plant produced everything from canned salmon to canned herring to cod liver oil capsules.

The fishing boats that tie up beside Canfisco are likely to be trawlers, identifiable by the large net drums toward the stern of the boat; gillnetters, with small drums toward the stern; or seiners, with the characteristic triangular pole structure used to close or purse the seine net. You may also see trollers, with several main fishing poles amidships and several more in the bow.

Walk through the Canfisco parking lot to the west for a view of the city's downtown and Canada Place. The contrast between the sturdy fish boats, rubber-aproned workers, and corrugated metal fish-packing plant, and the skyscrapers and glass to the west emphasize the dif-

Hastings Mill employees boasted of British Columbia "toothpicks," the enormous timbers shipped from the mill to ports around the world. This photograph was taken in 1890. (BCARS 12912).

ference between the working port from Canfisco east and the pleasure port on the far side of the harbour, where cruise ships dock and tourists stroll.

Retrace your steps to Dunlevy Street, and turn left, toward the water. The bright blue and white building across the street **(11)** is now the home of the Flying Angel Seamen's Club, a mission to seamen. This chapter of the building's life began after the National Harbours Board moved to new headquarters, but this is, in fact, the last on-site reminder of the first mill and wharf to operate on the south shore of Burrard Inlet. Founded in 1865 by Edward Stamp, Hastings Mill operated here independently, then as part of B.C. Mills, Timber and Trading Company until the National Harbours Board took over the site in the 1920s.

The building itself was erected in 1905—literally erected, not built—since it is one of BCMT&T's prefabricated houses, a show home from the priciest end of the line. Edwin C. Mahoney, manager of Royal City Mills, a branch of BCMT&T, put together this prefab system; the company then marketed the line heavily across Canada and the United States. The clapboard-panelled buildings, with doors and windows included, were the first prefabricated structures intended as permanent rather than temporary housing. They included simple and more elaborate houses, churches, schools, and business offices. To impress potential buyers, mill workers panelled each room of this house in a different kind of wood. Look for vertical battens on outside walls, marking the end of each prefab panel.

A sculpture beside the house commemorates Hastings Mill.

Railway, Alexander, and Heatley Streets

Turn back up Dunlevy, cross the tracks, then make an immediate left east on Railway Street, and follow Railway to Alexander Street. Railway Street here is devoted to warehouses; watch for trucks and other traffic. The street contains various wholesale warehouses, some of them belonging to Chinese produce wholesalers.

The area just south of here, along the 500 and 600 blocks of Alexander Street, was Vancouver's red-light district for a brief time. Although the first prostitutes arrived with the CPR gangs in 1885, Vancouver residents and police never lost the ambivalent attitude that still exists today. Both know the sex trade will not easily be eradicated, people don't want it in their own neighbourhood. Pressure from residents in each area prostitutes moved to brought about another move a year or a decade later: Alexander Street was chosen after police chased the women away from East Georgia near Main in 1911. The House of All Nations on Alexander was known as the house where "you can get everything from a chocolate-coloured damsel to a Swedish girl." The name of a madam is still inlaid in tile inside one of the entranceways—unfortunately not accessible to the public—in this block.

In 1912, the police were ordered to clean up the area, and the women moved to Pender Street. At the same time, the American Can Company began building a factory and warehouse on Railway where it meets Alexander. The building, completed in 1919, is the long, low, white construction ahead **(12)**, one of four plants considered industrial showpieces in the 1920s—though the steel tower with glass elevator cab is a product of a recent renovation. The can-manufacturing plant closed down in the 1980s; a major renovation that turned the building into combined

The refurbished American Can Company building at Railway and Alexander streets.

manufacturing, warehouse, and office space has won its designers two heritage restoration awards. The elevator tower and the sparkling white paint are the main external evidence of the renovation. Inside, a courtyard has been converted to an artistic atrium.

At the eastern end of the building is the second coming of a Vancouver institution. Anyone who loved to wander the old port area and watch the comings and goings of fishing boats and freighters knew about breakfast at the Marine View Coffee Shop, and was bereft when it was torn down. But the Marine View is back, in cleaner, brighter surroundings, with the same owner, same view of the port, and same plain, good food.

Opposite the American Can Company building is evidence of the rebirth of this part of Strathcona as a residential area: an apartment co-operative made up of new and renovated buildings, created by the Downtown Eastside Residents Association in 1985.

Walk under the Heatley Street overpass, then turn right and make a U-turn at the traffic light to follow Heatley Street over Alexander Street. This overpass provides a wide view of Vancouver's port facilities, with the harbour stretching on the left toward Canada Place, and on the right toward the Second Narrows Bridge. View the following from the top of the overpass, or take the stairs down from the overpass to the street below and follow the walkway beside the street to Ballantyne Pier **(13)**. Port of Vancouver plans call for the demolition of several of these buildings and the erection of new cruise ship facilities, so your decision to stay up top or descend may depend on the degree of chaos and construction.

To the right (east) from the overpass, you can see, immediately below and south of the tracks, what looks like a modern squatters' camp, a throwback to the time when the land to the east was known as Tar Flats and occupied by hundreds of transients. The rail tracks lead east toward grain elevators built after World War I to store prairie grain for freighters that would transport it to countries around the world.

To the left of the huge concrete elevators are various port facilities that illustrate modern bulk-loading techniques: giant cranes used to load containers onto freighters and bulk storage facilities. Across the tracks

The last days of Ballantyne Pier: bulldozers begin work on tearing down most of the 1920s pier sheds.

and just to the right of the overpass is Ballantyne Pier, "bloody Ballantyne" in the 1930s.

On June 18, 1935, a thousand striking/locked-out longshoremen marched on Ballantyne to evict strike-breakers from the docks. Mounted police waiting at the docks charged them, firing tear gas and swinging clubs. Twenty-eight were injured as the police chased the marchers back to Hastings, into homes and stores.

Ballantyne has seen both cargo and passengers aplenty since the four sheds now being torn down were built in the early 1920s. It was intended as a general cargo terminal; ships docking here handled grain—but also Japanese oranges, Okanagan apples, bonded liquor, automobiles, and steel pipe. In the years immediately after World War II, ships from Germany, Sweden, and the Netherlands brought thousands of Europeans to Vancouver and to Ballantyne Pier.

Labour strife, though still present, is now less violent; most immigrants arrive by air; and the port requires updated cruise ship and cargo facilities. The façade and about one third of Shed 1 will be retained in rebuilding Ballantyne. New buildings will house a forest products terminal, warehousing mainly pulp and top-end lumber, while cruise ships unable to find a berth at Canada Place will dock alongside. A walkway will lead passengers to the front of the terminal. Once construction is completed, walkers will be able to see ships and pier facilities from a viewpoint at the east end of the terminal.

Make a U-turn, and walk south on Heatley Street. On the right (west) side of Heatley from Cordova to Hastings, you can see rooming houses and houses converted to apartments, common in this part of Strathcona. You may also see a modern version of something much older: streetwalking prostitutes. Brothels were located east of Heatley before 1900; in 1913, Vancouver police closed brothels, and women took their business to the streets, a custom that continues today.

Strathcona: The Residential Area

Cross Hastings (if traffic is heavy, you may wish to detour a block east or west, to a traffic light) and continue south

on Heatley. The mainly residential part of Strathcona begins south of Hastings. The row of six houses on the right (west) side of Heatley between Hastings and Pender **(14)**, unrestored but attractive in pastel paints, was built around the turn of the century as rental accommodation. Once almost identical, the houses have been modified: only one retains a shaded verandah, while the verandahs on the others have been walled in to provide extra living or storage space, and the original clapboard has been replaced on some of the houses with shingles.

Turn left (east) on Pender Street. On the southeast corner of Pender and Heatley stands what was once the Schara Tzedeck Synagogue **(15)**, completed in 1921. Jews were among the earliest immigrants to British Columbia, arriving with the first gold-rushers in 1858. Around the turn of the century, more Jewish immigrants came to Vancouver, many of them Orthodox Jews. Most settled in Strathcona; they built their first small synagogue on this corner just before World War I, replacing it with this building after the war. As they moved into other areas of the city after World War II, a synagogue was built farther south, and this building sold. The new owner converted the old building to a gymnasium, then gave it to the Vancouver Boys' Club. Its interior rebuilt, it has been converted into condominiums and renamed Alexander Court, still with the original exterior and dome.

The Ukrainian Cultural Centre **(16)**, a block east at the corner of East Pender and Hawks Avenue, reflects the story of another immigrant group. In the 1920s and

Staff of the United Church Women's Missionary Society headquarters in Strathcona, in 1924. (BCARS 29048)

1930s, this area of Strathcona was solidly Ukrainian. Ukrainian immigrants who settled in Vancouver generally hewed to one of two political philosophies: some were socialists or supporters of communism; others were strongly nationalistic (for the Ukrainian nation, that is) and equally strongly opposed to Russian Communist rule of their homeland.

The socialistic Society of Ukrainian Workers and Farmers erected this building as the Ukrainian Farmer-Labour Temple in 1928. The hall rang to the music and speeches of people who termed themselves progressive. In 1938, after police evicted unemployed men occupying the Vancouver post office, the building served as a hospital for those beaten or gassed in the eviction.

When the German and Soviet governments signed a pact and Canada went to war against Germany in 1939, the Canadian government outlawed all Communist organizations. The temple was confiscated and sold to the Ukrainian Greek Orthodox Church for a tiny sum. When, two years later, Canada and the Soviet Union became allies, the previous owners demanded their building back; it was returned in 1945. After the war, the conflict between supporters of the Communist regime and Ukrainian nationalists continued. The left-leaning group that owns this building has now declined as Ukrainian nationalism takes wing once more.

Next door is the Lesya Ukrainka housing project.

These blocks of Pender Street underline the real victory won when most of Strathcona was saved from urban redevelopment. A great variety of housing styles, crowded closely together, creates the area's characteristic streetscape. Many houses date from the turn of the century; their verandahs and bay windows contrast nicely with the modern architecture of new townhouses. As elsewhere in the area, some houses are well below street level, others well above. In the 1890s, the city began a street-levelling program, ironing out hills and filling dips, so that some houses ended up below, some above, the street level. You can also see the narrow, 7.6-metre lots common in Strathcona.

Turn right on Campbell Avenue and walk south. Before the False Creek flats were drained, canoeists could follow this route from Burrard Inlet to False Creek at high tide. After the area was drained, the interurban tram line ran along Campbell. The bland and boring rabbit warren of Stamps Place **(17)**, part of the Raymur housing project, across Campbell at the end of Pender Street, underlines the victory won by the neighbourhood activists who saved much of Strathcona from this kind of urban renewal.

Sacred Heart Catholic Church, at Campbell and Keefer, shows the changing ethnic lines of Strathcona. In the 1920s and 1930s, Sacred Heart parishioners were largely Italian. A name plaque in Italian remains from those days. Now, it is one of half a dozen Chinese Christian churches in Strathcona, including Catholic, Mennonite, Basel Hakka Lutheran, and Christ Church of China.

Chinese who came to Canada before World War I often found more solace in their fraternal organizations than in organized religion. "The Chinese are generally a sceptical race," a Chinese Canadian born in Canada of Chinese parents wrote in 1936. He could not say what religion he was, for he read "the Bible for inspiration and moral guidance, the Stoic Creed for courage, Confucianism for ethics, the Epicurean Philosophy for enjoyment, Christian Science for right thinking, and Physical Culture for developing a sound body." Later comers were more likely to be members of a religious denomination: Chinese churches, most of which conduct services in Mandarin, Cantonese, and sometimes Fukinese, are scattered throughout the Lower Mainland.

Across Campbell Street is the stalwart architecture of the Russian People's Home **(18)**. When this building opened in

1937, it was the Croatian Education Home: opening ceremonies included a Croatian Tamburitza orchestra. But when many Croatians returned to Croatia after World War II to help rebuild their homeland, the building was sold to the Federation of Russian Canadians, a left-leaning organization that sponsored cultural and political activities, including movie nights, dances, and entertainment for visiting Russian sailors. The collapse of the Soviet Union has eaten into the group's support. The Ukrainian Services Centre also operates out of this building.

Many Strathcona residents kept chickens and cows. Look into the alley running west from Campbell between Keefer and East Georgia to see several of the pens that used to house livestock, converted now to garages and storage sheds.

A church a block farther south on Campbell Street shows the other side of the Russian political coin. One hundred families fled the Russian revolution in 1917, arriving in Vancouver via Manchuria. Joining them throughout the 1920s and 1930s were other anti-communist Russian refugees, among them Rev. Alexander Kizuin. Kizuin financed the Holy Trinity Russian Orthodox Church at 710 Campbell Avenue **(19)** almost single-handedly, working on it himself and donating the cost of the building materials. He died in 1953; the church was abandoned until the Gorelik family bought it and converted it into a church used mainly by members of their family.

Turn right (west) on Union Street. The houses along this block of Union again show the effects of the street-

The brilliant white of Holy Trinity Russian Orthodox Church, on Campbell Avenue.

levelling program in Strathcona. This time, they are above grade, reached by flights of steps that lead upward from the sidewalk. Close to the end of the block, a small grocery store makes its own comment on the neighbourhood: it sells homemade bread, not only by the loaf but by the half and quarter loaf, for the single people on a strict budget who live in the district. Next door, stretching south from the corner of Union and Hawks, is a long row of attached housing built between 1900 and 1910, primarily as rental accommodation for the families of longshoremen, clerks, and other workers who lived in Strathcona, or as hostels for single working men.

Turn right (north) on Hawks Avenue. The neat green row of attached houses on your right **(20)**, with their

Street-levelling programs in Strathcona have left some houses well below street level, others well above.

bright red trim and fences, look very different from the row housing south of Union, but early photographs show the two buildings were quite similar. In the 1970s, the red and green building, once a hostel, was renovated and is an example of good urban renewal in Strathcona, with balconies cut into the roof, façades spruced up, and fences and new paint added.

This block provides several demonstrations of how older housing can be preserved and restored. Across the street at 701–725 Hawks is another run of row housing, renovated and painted bright blue in the 1980s. Take a look here and elsewhere at the attractive, half-wild perennial gardens planted between the houses and the street.

Continue through the mini-park along Hawks to

Turn-of-the-century row housing at Hawks and Union streets.

Keefer Street. At Hawks and Keefer is MacLean Park, the replacement for the original MacLean Park taken over for the first urban renewal housing built in the 1960s. Houses, apartment buildings, and a bakery were torn down to make room for the new park. Several chestnut and maple trees remain from the homes that used to occupy the block.

To the right (east) on Keefer are two tall houses. Number 856 was built in 1892, 860 in 1894; they were part of the building boom in Strathcona in the 1890s. North of Keefer on Hawks (502–520 Hawks) are four houses built as rental units in 1900. In the 1980s, a group of determined people bought and restored the four, and rebuilt two houses that were part of the original group of six. The first tenants in the houses included a sea captain, a butcher, and the circulation manager of the *Province* newspaper.

Across the street from these houses, at 507, 515, and 521 Hawks **(21)**, are the earliest-known, still-standing prefabricated houses from the B.C. Mills, Timber and Trading Company. Like the old Hastings Mill office at the foot of Dunlevy, these houses rolled off the lumber lines in two- and four-foot clapboard panels. Unlike the mill office, these houses were built for people to live in, and were probably prototypes of the prefab system patented in 1904. Look for the battens that separate the prefabricated wall panels.

The house at the southeast corner of Keefer and Hawks was once the Montreal Bakery. On the northwest corner, a small store occupies the corner of a 1906 apartment building.

Keefer Street, Hawks to Columbia

Turn left (west) on Keefer Street, and walk back toward Chinatown. Keefer in this block contains a good mixture of housing: old and unrestored, old and restored, new but still in keeping with the streetscape.

Above street level in the next block are the playing fields of Strathcona School, the wire-mesh fencing screening St. Francis Xavier Church a block away. On the left is an indication of the changing nature of the Asian community in Vancouver: Vietnamese immigrants have claimed this small building as the Vietnamese Alliance Church.

Strathcona School **(22)** was one of the first schools in Vancouver; its first building, long demolished, was completed in 1891. The brick building facing Keefer Street dates from 1897, other wings and buildings from the 1920s. Students of some fifty nationalities gave the school the reputation of a miniature United Nations. Said one ex-student, "We all knew each other's swear words." The ethnic mix still exists at Strathcona, though now more students are of Asian and fewer of European origin.

Students in the 1930s, at Strathcona School, show the varied ethnic backgrounds of Strathcona residents. (CVA Sch. P 116)

The Bodhi Rey Tsang Buddhist Temple on Keefer Street.

At the corner of Princess and Keefer, a turreted and gingerbreaded house stands, built in 1900 for Gregory Tom, the first principal of Strathcona School. Anecdote suggests that he supervised the playgrounds from his turret. The Strathcona Community Centre, on the school grounds, provides multilingual services to Strathcona residents.

In the 500-block Keefer is the orange Bodhi Rey Tsang Temple **(23)**, operated by the Poo Tee Town Buddhist Society. The temple is open every day from 10 a.m. to 4 p.m.

In the next block of Keefer, stretching south, are the buildings of the first urban renewal project in Strathcona, the apartment buildings and townhouses erected on the site of MacLean Park **(24)**. Few Chinese Strathcona resi-

Harsh walls and stucco in the MacLean Park housing project on Keefer Street.

dents wanted to move into this sterile development. Said one, "You can take the cement cubicle and stick it in your ear. You want to take my house and put me in one of them cubicles? *You* go in there."

A block later, across Gore Street, Keefer enters Chinatown. This block between Gore and Main contains a mixture of stores and other buildings; a new bank building shares the block with turn-of-the-century hotels. Here too is "bakery row," a series of Chinese bakeries. Those who look in the windows may get a shock: instead of what they think of as Chinese pastries, they see display cases filled with fancy creations that look exactly like French pastries. And well they should. When China was forcibly opened to western interests in the nineteenth century,

Chinese vegetable dealers lined up every day on Keefer Street in the 1930s. (CVA 492-45)

French pastry chefs travelled to China to demonstrate their art. Chinese chefs adopted and adapted: the pastries they bake are similar to French ones, but less sweet. Also on display are almond cookies and other Chinese savouries and sweets.

In this block, as in some other blocks of Chinatown, is an herbalist, who will find an herbal remedy for whatever ails you. These herbal prescriptions are blended to balance the yin (cold) and yang (hot) forces that must be properly balanced in the body for good health. Prescriptions include roots, herbs, and animal parts. A tea company at the corner of Keefer and Main **(25)** offers a wide variety of teas, regular and herbal; ask to sample a cup of the variety of the day.

In the Dr. Sun Yat-Sen Park, Chinatown.

Follow Keefer Street across Main to Columbia Street.
The False Creek mud flats once came almost up to Pender Street. The flats were drained in 1909, and tracks laid to the Great Northern Railway station at Columbia and Pender.

Cross Columbia (no crosswalk here, so you may want to go to the corner of Pender and backtrack) and walk into Dr. Sun Yat-Sen Park (26), open 10 a.m. to 4 p.m. Entrance to the park is free; the classical garden next door charges an entrance fee. The park and garden were built in the early 1980s by artisans brought from China, who modelled the garden on a Ming Dynasty scholar's garden; the building materials also come from China. The garden is said to be the only one of its kind outside

China. The central courtyard is a pavilion with water-eroded limestone from Lake Tai; the Double Corridor zigzags to discourage evil spirits. The Jade Water Pavilion is a place of singular peace, a perfect spot to end this walking tour.

FURTHER READING

Griffin, Kevin. *Vancouver's Many Faces.* Vancouver: Whitecap Books, 1993. History and background of ethnic communities in the city.

Kalman, Harold; Ron Phillips; and Robin Ward. *Exploring Vancouver: The Essential Architectural Guide.* Vancouver: UBC Press, 1993. Architectural background on a number of East Side buildings.

Kluckner, Michael, and John Atkin. *Heritage Walks Around Vancouver.* Vancouver: Whitecap Books, 1992. Includes short Strathcona and downtown East Side tours.

Marlatt, Daphne, and Carole Itter. *Opening Doors: Vancouver's East End.* Victoria: Province of British Columbia, Sound Heritage Series, vol. VIII, 1 and 2, 1979. Oral history of the east end, including interesting interviews with East Side residents.

ACKNOWLEDGEMENTS

THANKS GO TO the staffs of the Vancouver City Archives, the British Columbia Archives and Records Services, and the Vancouver Public Library. Special thanks to Glenn Drexhage and Joe Thompson, for their endurance.